EXPANDING AMERICA

Seward's Folly and Alaska

Hex Kleinmartin

Cavendish
Square

New York

Published in 2016 by Cavendish Square Publishing, LLC
243 5th Avenue, Suite 136, New York, NY 10016
Copyright © 2016 by Cavendish Square Publishing, LLC

First Edition

Website: cavendishsq.com

This publication represents the opinions and views of the author based on his or her personal
experience, knowledge, and research. The information in this book serves as a general guide only.
The author and publisher have used their best efforts in preparing this book and disclaim liability rising
directly or indirectly from the use and application of this book.

CPSIA Compliance Information: Batch #CW16CSQ

All websites were available and accurate when this book was sent to press.

Library of Congress Cataloging-in-Publication Data

Kleinmartin, Hex, author.
Seward's Folly and Alaska / Hex Kleinmartin.
pages cm. — (Expanding America)
Includes bibliographical references and index.
ISBN 978-1-5026-0970-0 (hardcover) ISBN 978-1-5026-0971-7 (ebook)
1. Alaska—History—Juvenile literature. I. Title.

F904.3.K55 2016
979.8—dc23

2015027440

Editorial Director: David McNamara
Editors: Andrew Coddington and Kelly Spence
Copy Editor: Rebecca Rohan
Art Director: Jeffrey Talbot
Designers: Amy Greenan and Stephanie Flecha
Senior Production Manager: Jennifer Ryder-Talbot
Production Editor: Renni Johnson
Photo Research: J8 Media

The photographs in this book are used by permission and through the courtesy of: Everett Historical/
Shutterstock.com, cover; Mattalia/Shutterstock.com, cover background and used throughout the
book; Leutze, Emanuel Gottlieb/Private Collection/Bridgeman Images, 6; Carol Highsmith/Library
of Congress, 8; Library of Congress, 9, 10, 11, 12, 32, 34, 46, 53, 57, 59, 60; Boston Public Library/
Chart of the Northern Passage between Asia & America (8249585867).jpg/Wikimedia Commons, 15;
Woodville, Richard Caton II/Private Collection/Bridgeman Images, 24-25; National Archives, 35; Public
Domain/Berings ships wrecked.jpg/Wikimedia Commons, 36; Public Domain/Geographicus Rare
Antique Maps/1762 Janvier Map of North America (Sea of the West) - Geographicus - NorthAmerica-
janvier-1762.jpg/Wikimedia Commons, 39; Public Domain/Flag of the Russian-American Company,
1806.tiff/Wikimedia Commons, 42; Public Domain/Nortwestern America - Alaska in 1867.jpg/Wikimedia
Commons, 47; Edward Curtis/Library of Congress, 49; North Wind Picture Archives, 50; Public Domain/
USFW/Prudhoe Bay oil fields 1971 FWS.jpg/Wikimedia Commons, 64; Dennis Hellawell/Library of
Congress, 71; Joseph Sohm/Shutterstock.com, 76.

Printed in the United States of America

CONTENTS

Alaska, the Controversy

I n the history of the United States, the acquisition of Alaska is important, but like so many other occurrences in United States history, a few simple facts don't do it justice. Many people will be able to tell you that in 1867, William H. Seward agreed to purchase Alaska from Russia, which is true, but it doesn't tell the whole story. To really understand the complexities of the situation, you have to look at what was going on not just in the United States at the time but also on the rest of the world stage.

As much as George Washington admonished his presidential successors to "avoid foreign entanglements" and James Monroe would declare that the Americas would take care of themselves without European interference (what would become known as the Monroe Doctrine), this was still a time when European powers held territory and influence in the Americas. Often, when we think of these in the early years of United States history, we think of the French, the English, and the Spanish being involved. However, in this occurrence, we will see how much influence Russia had in the international community.

As you read this book, remember that all the decisions, policies, brokering, and sometimes even underhanded dealings that went on in history happened because of the motivations of people just as real as *you* are. Certainly, they lived in their own times and their minds were shaped by what was going on in the world around them, but they had loves, fears, desires, and hatreds. They made mistakes, and likely, some of them felt regrets after the actions were taken. And whether you know it or not, it's likely that the United States' purchase of Alaska from the Russians in 1867 has affected your life in some way.

Chapter 1 is a summary of the Alaska Purchase, looking at what the event included, where and when it happened, and why it should be considered an important event in the history of the United States. Chapter 2 will explain the circumstances surrounding the Purchase, and the way that the United States was looking at the world around it to see where it could benefit. It also explains who was involved with making the Purchase happen (or trying to stop it from happening), and why they chose to acquire Alaska in the way that they did. Chapter 3 provides an overview of the area itself from the perspectives of the explorers, both before and after the event, and an examination of the explorers themselves, the challenges they overcame to make their discoveries, and what it was they found. Chapter 4 tells the story of the settlers who inevitably came and helped to make Alaska a working part of the United States— both who they were, and what the event meant to them. And lastly, Chapter 5 examines what the Alaska Purchase meant for the United States in the time that followed it. This includes both a historical factor in looking at the more immediate results for the country, but also what the area means to the United States, and the world, today.

"Baron" Eduard de Stoeckl, the Russian emissary who negotiated the sale of the Alaska Territory

CHAPTER ONE

Buying Alaska

Situated in the extreme northwest of the North American continent is the state of Alaska. Of all the fifty states, it is the largest, covering 663,268 square miles (1,717,856 square kilometers), and is the farthest north and also the farthest west. Alaska is also home to North America's tallest mountain, Denali (Mount McKinley), which stands 20,321 feet (6,194 meters) high; and has the lowest population density, at 1.26 people per square mile (0.49 people per sq km). Its climates range from arctic **tundra** in the north to **maritime** rainforest in the south, and it has almost 34,900 miles (54,700 kilometers) of coastline—more than all the other United States combined. Alaska also contains about 16,120 square miles (26,000 sq km) of **glaciers** and more than three million lakes. Alaska's approximately twelve thousand rivers and streams collectively give it 364,200 miles (587,400 km) of waterways.

Alaska has both volcanic mountains, in the south and along the Aleutians, and mountains created by tectonic plates colliding, folding, and pushing the rock layers up, in the

Areas of Alaska are very lush with plants and wildlife, like this area of the Chugach National Forest.

Alaska Range where Denali is found. Because of this, it is rich in mineral wealth, but Alaska also has lumber, animal, and fish life, as well as petroleum, all in abundance.

Another important fact about Alaska is that it is separated from Russia by the Bering **Strait**, a waterway that is only 51 miles (82 km) wide at its narrowest spot. It is no wonder that the **Imperial** Russians claimed the area for themselves, colonizing and trading there as a chartered **monopoly** for the rich profits of the fur trade.

As rich as we now know Alaska is, in the 1860s most of what was known about it was its coastline, and the wealth of seals and sea otters that could be hunted for their furs. Almost one-third of all the land in the Alaska Territory was above the **Arctic Circle**, and residents experienced midnight sun in the summer and polar night in the winter.

Settlers had made forays up several of the major rivers, and some inland trading posts had been started, but the fur trade was trailing off, and the profits for Russian business interests were dwindling against the costs. In the meantime, Russia was acquiring more Asian land, which was easier to control and defend. What Russia needed was someone to buy the area.

The Americans wanted that North American land, at least before the British in Canada got ahold of it. The British wanted it, too, but at that point in time, the Russians were none too happy with the British due to some misplaced

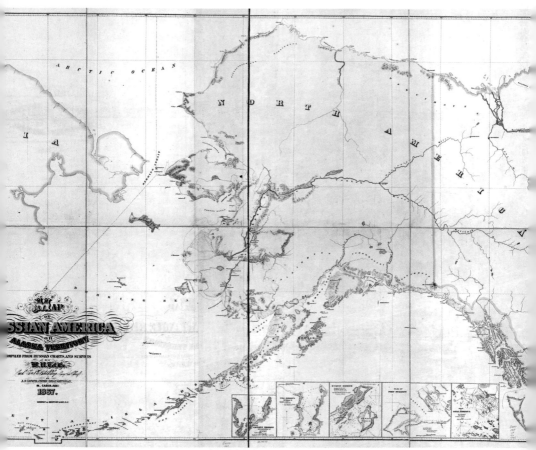

An 1867 map of the Alaska Territory; note how little is known of the interior.

trusts and a war. They were looking to deal with someone else, such as the Americans, who had within the last ninety years been in not one but two wars against the British.

The Players

Not all Americans thought Alaska was a worthwhile purchase. While William H. Seward thought it important to try to gather more land for Americans to expand into, and brokered the deal to buy the Alaska Territory for the United States, some people thought Seward was taking advantage of President Johnson, or even that he undertook the deal completely on his own. However, things were more complex than that, as the United States was recovering from the Civil War, and Russia was looking for ways to simplify after the reforms that followed the Crimean War were instituted.

Левицкій
на Мойкѣ, 30. С. Петербургъ.

Tsar Alexander II, Emperor of Russia

Tsar Alexander II freed the serfs in much the same way that Lincoln had freed the slaves, but this led to social turmoil, economic troubles, and issues where infrastructure within the Russian Empire was lacking. Dealing with Alaska, and the British Hudson's Bay Trading Company's encroachment on the Alaska Territory's resources, was just too much extra to deal with for what it was worth. In 1866, the tsar sent Eduard de Stoeckl—who

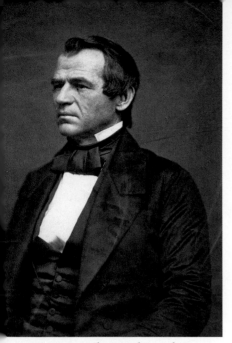

US President Andrew Johnson

called himself a baron but had no credentials of aristocracy—as Russia's ambassador to talk with Seward about the sale. This kind of discussion had come up before, in 1859, but at that time the internal issues of the United States that led up to the Civil War seemed much more important to American political officials than buying the Alaska Territory. However, the climate in Washington, and indeed the whole country, was full of pitfalls from both political figures with their own ambitions and business owners who were looking out for their own profits. It was in this swirling mess that a few key people made the deal happen by working to keep the right people happy, and playing up the right interests to others, and by keeping the money involved at what was a reasonable and acceptable level.

Now, given all these issues and troubles, how did it come to be that in 1867 the United States acquired the Alaska Territory, and what did it mean for Americans?

US Secretary of State William H. Seward, who acted as the US broker for the sale of the Alaska Territory

CHAPTER TWO

People and Events That Led Up to the Purchase

Looking at Russia's sale of Alaska to the United States and trying to find out why things happened the way they did means looking at not just the sale but at what was going on beforehand. This includes looking at a scope of area outside of the Northwest of North America, at events happening in many different places in the world.

Russian Furs

It really was no surprise that Russia claimed the Alaska Territory initially. It was not until 1640 that the Russians conquered what we now know as Siberia, and they started exploring this new conquest. The fur trade was one of the lucrative industries that they capitalized on in the later 1600s and 1700s. The newly acquired areas of Siberia they controlled offered opportunities for many furs, and native trappers who survived the conquest could pay their taxes in furs. This was a preferable arrangement as the natives did not have a money economy and did a much better job at hunting good quality furs than the Russian soldiers.

During this time, China was the biggest market for Russian furs, and it was nearby. While many Europeans wanted Russian sable furs for coats, the Chinese were happy with squirrel pelts for jackets. Thus, the relatively accepting Chinese market made practically all types of fur profitable, so long as transporting them didn't get too expensive. As there were few roads in the area for caravans of carts or wagons, but streams, rivers, and oceans were in good supply, water-based transport became the obvious way to make a fortune in furs. Coastal peoples, or those who lived near the mouths of rivers or along good, protected, natural harbors, became the logical trading partners of the Russian fur traders.

Being that North America was so close, and the Aleutian Islands stretch out toward the east coast of Russia, this was a logical place to continue exploration and trade. Here, of course, there was plenty of coastline from the islands, but as Russians got to North America and traveled down the Northwestern coast, they discovered more and bigger islands, bays, **fjords**, and navigable rivers. The great bulk of Russian exploration was done on the coastal areas, and it was only later that forays into Alaska's great, expansive interior were made.

The Natives did not like the Russians' presence and began to fight back against the Russian encroachment and rule toward the beginning of the 1800s. As a result, the fur trade started to decline in profitability. The Russians began

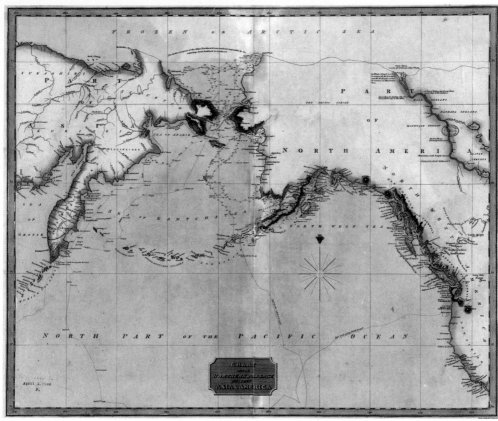

This map shows eastern Russia and the Alaska Territory, with the location of the Aleutian Islands prominently shown between the two.

to see Alaska less as a moneymaking colony and more as an area that needed to be taken care of. Both the British in Canada and the Americans farther south along the coast had better resources and more forces in the area, and the thought was that one final profit could be turned to the Russian advantage by selling this huge piece of land to one of these two nations. In fact, Grand Duke Konstantin Nikolaevich postulated a view that the Americans who were spreading quickly across the continent would soon take control of the whole of North America, and that Russia should at least receive payment for giving up their colony before they simply lost it.

The British were the obvious choice, though. They already had a Hudson's Bay Trading Company post within the borders of the Alaska Territory at Fort Yukon, and agents trading in the eastern areas that bordered what is now British Columbia. Britain had been making diplomatic overtures to the Russians about the acquisition of Alaskan lands up until the 1850s, but at that time the area was still too important to the Russians to **relinquish**. Also, the world picture in the middle of the nineteenth century was one of turmoil, with Russia right in the midst of things.

China's Influences

During the 1840s, Russia's Asian fur-trading partner, China, was in trouble. While there was great demand in Europe for Chinese goods, such as silk, tea, and porcelain, they were hard to acquire. China had a "closed-door" trading policy, which meant there were only thirteen Chinese companies that Europeans could trade with and only in the city of Canton. The policy also dictated that the only European goods that these items could be traded for was silver. As the other Chinese people were kept out of this trade, this monopoly served as a gatekeeping system, and European items were hardly known in most of China.

In an attempt to recoup some of the lost British silver, the British East India Company had started to sell Indian-grown and processed **opium** for silver, both directly and to non–East India Company European traders. These traders would transport it to places along the Chinese coast and sell it to the Chinese there. Networks of middlemen in China brought opium in and took the silver back out. By 1838, the British East India Company was selling almost 1,400 tons (1,270 metric tons) of opium to British and American traders who were then feeding it into China. As the Chinese government noted the growing number of addicts and the depletion of silver currency within China, the emperor reacted to stop the damaging trade quickly.

In 1839, just over 1,200 tons (1,088 t) of opium were seized from foreign traders, and the traders, along with non-opium trading merchants, were placed under house arrest. The opium was publicly destroyed and trade with those outside China stopped, as Chinese warships blockaded ports and patrolled the coasts. The Chinese also demanded that all foreign traders sign a bond that they would not traffic opium, a demand that the British government objected to. When a Quaker vessel agreed to sign the bond, against British wishes, British naval vessels blockaded the Pearl River. When a second British ship attempted to sail up the river, the naval vessels fired a warning shot. Official Chinese naval records report that Chinese ships sailed to protect the trader, and the First Opium War began as British and Chinese ships fought.

In this encounter, and in other land and naval battles, British steamships and rifle-barreled guns showed the technological superiority of the British military over the Chinese forces. Cities, ports, forts, and even the Imperial tax barges were easily captured by the British. The Treaty of Nanking between the British and the Chinese, signed in August of 1842, was an unequal treaty. It gave more to the British: more ports were opened to trade, notably Shanghai; Hong Kong was "given" to the British; and the Chinese had to pay indemnities and were generally humiliated on the world stage. Yet this was just the start of troubles for Russia's southeastern neighbor.

The 1850s saw the start of the Taiping Rebellion in China. A mix of discontent with the rulers in power during the First Opium War and the rise of Hong Xiuquan, a charismatic leader who claimed to be the younger brother of Jesus, led to the uprising. It embodied a replacement of well-entrenched ideologies with a version of Christianity and concepts of "common ownership" as one sees in communism. Starting in the 1840s, Xiuquan's sect gained public support in local areas by suppressing bandits and pirates. As the government officials tried to stop the sect, they gained even more support, and fought back against the government with guerrilla warfare.

By 1851, the fighting was direct, and government forces were forced out of some cities and military positions. By 1856, the rebels had an army that included women and may have numbered as many as five hundred thousand. They held Zhejiang and Jiangxi provinces entirely, and nearly half of Hubei, Anhui, and Jiangsu provinces, ruling as many as thirty million people. It was only an unsuccessful attempt in 1860 to conquer Shanghai that finally brought European forces into the fight. By 1864, Imperial Chinese forces had retaken the rebel areas, but the fighting was bloody. It has been estimated that over the fifteen years of the rebellion, between twenty and thirty million soldiers' and civilians' deaths could be attributed to it. As one might guess, this was a fragile time for the Imperial government of China.

Russia's Benefits from Unequal Treaties

Many unequal treaties with China, where military force was used as a threat to make the Chinese give concessions to the other treaty member, occurred as a result of this instability. Two of them were very important to the Russians' interest in the Alaska Territory. The first was the 1858 Treaty of Aigun, which ceded the land between the Stanovoy Mountains and the Amur River to Russia, an area of over 231,660 square miles (600,000 sq km). This gave Russia its much-desired ice-free Pacific water access and opened up trade all along the new border. The treaty was accomplished by the Russian military gathering tens of thousands of troops on the border of Mongolia and Manchuria as an implicit threat of invasion. The second occurred during the 1860 Convention of Peking, where the Russians intruded on the negotiations the British and French were having to stop the Second Opium War, which had culminated with the burning of imperial estates (the original target of the burning had been the Forbidden City, but the Europeans thought its destruction would harm treaty negotiations). The Russian dignitary sat in on the treaty signing and was able to benefit from the treaty, as China ceded parts of Outer Mongolia to Russia, thus giving them 64,100 square miles (165,900 sq km) of new land on the Pacific Coast, which included the natural harbors and abundant natural resources there. It is here that Vladivostok would be founded in August 1860; it would eventually become the naval base for the Russian Pacific fleet.

These changes in new Pacific coastal territories that were readily land-accessible to the Russian military made the travel and defense costs of the resources of the Alaska Territory much less viable. Furthermore, with the Chinese market being further opened by these treaties, furs were losing importance to other trade goods found elsewhere in Russia. But where furs were still desired, they could be procured on these new Russian coasts of Asia.

How the Ottoman Empire Affected the Purchase of Alaska

With all of this turmoil and change with China, it would seem that those longstanding British suggestions of purchasing Alaska would have been quickly taken up by the

Russians, and yet they were not. To look at why, we must look at another part of the world where there was yet more turmoil that involved Russia during the 1850s: the areas around the Black Sea, to the southwest of Russia.

The major player on the world stage in this area was the **Ottoman Empire**. Founded in 1299 and reaching its highest point of power and control by the 1500s, the Ottoman Empire of the early 1800s was stagnant and in decline. Tsar Nicholas I is said to have spoken to a British ambassador about the Ottoman Empire as "a man gravely ill" who essentially needed his affairs put in order before it was too late. The British Ambassador took this conversation to mean that the tsar had plans to take over the Ottoman Empire as it became more and more vulnerable. By the time this was relayed back to Britain, however, Russia's attempts to conquer the Ottoman Empire were already in play. Russia was already involved in European affairs due to its place in the Holy Alliance of 1815, a coalition of Prussia, Austria, and Russia whose aim was to counter European threats to aristocratic stability and threats of secularism after the devastation suffered during the French Revolutionary Wars. Trying to keep down republican governments, Russia intervened in things like the Hungarian Revolution of 1848, being called the "gendarme (policeman) of Europe."

One of the reasons for this view of Russia's place in Europe was that after the Russo-Turkish War (1768–1774), the Russians had secured freedom to worship for Christians living in the the Ottoman-controlled provinces of Wallachia and Moldavia, and had the right to enforce that within the Ottoman areas if necessary. In this way, Russia held a place as protector of the Christians within the Ottoman Empire, though for some in Catholic France, the idea of having an Orthodox Christian Russia as the protector of the Christian Holy Lands didn't sit well.

Napoleon III capitalized on this in 1853, when he was influenced by the clerical party to appoint a strong, outspoken Catholic to the post of ambassador to the Ottoman Empire. Upon acceptance, the Ottomans would recognize France as the protector of the Christians there. This would then give France control over all of the important Christian churches and shrines in Jerusalem. It was thought that to other Catholic nations of Europe this would heighten the prestige of France, but the one certain thing that it did was to upset Russia when the Ottoman Empire accepted the ambassador.

The Russian ambassador Admiral Alexander Sergeyevich Menschikov pointed out to the Ottomans that they had treaties and years of precedent of being the protector of the Christians in the Empire. The Ottomans agreed with this, renounced the agreement with the French, and formally restated that the Russians were indeed the protectors of the Christians within the Empire. While this action was satisfactory for the Russians, now the French were upset.

Napoleon III took this as an affront to French power and responded in force. He sent the newly refitted ship of the line—the biggest of broadside warships, the historical equivalent of our modern battleships—*Charlemagne* to the Black Sea to demonstrate to the Ottomans that France was a power not to be trifled with. The *Charlemagne* was fitted with eighty cannons and just two years before had been reworked to fit a steam engine that could push her along at a speed of nearly nine knots. The Ottoman navy had seven steam-powered ships at the time, five of which were paddle-wheel frigates or corvettes that were susceptible to broadsides from a ship of the line.

The presence of the French ship, combined with forceful diplomacy and economic threats and bribes, was impressive. Helped along by the British working to bolster the French cause by giving Russia and the Ottomans different versions of the truth and different assurances, the Ottomans once again recognized the French as the protector of the Christians. However, the presence of a French warship in the Black Sea was a breach of the London Straits Convention of 1841, which kept all warships—barring Ottomans and wartime allies of the Ottomans—from sailing through the Turkish Straits between the Black Sea and the Mediterranean Sea. It seemed a challenge to Russia, whose Black Sea fleet could not sail to the Mediterranean Sea because of the agreement.

When Menschikov realized that he was making no progress with the Ottomans, he returned to St. Petersburg to report to the tsar. The Russians felt they were failing while France continued to gain ground. The tsar was frustrated by the lack of success. He decided to determine the strength of the Ottoman Empire's forces and the degree of Britain's resolve to resist Russia's encroachment. In order to test this, he ordered several thousand troops to invade Turkish Moldavia and Wallachia, areas that were under the protection of the Ottoman Empire but were for the most part autonomous.

Unfortunately, this proved to have further ramifications than just a test to gauge the Empire's and Britain's responses, as all the treaties that had been made by European nations with the Ottomans as well as the Russians now threatened the peace of almost all of Europe (much as World War I would nearly sixty years later). This pushed both Britain and France into a quick response on the side of the Ottomans, in order to try and keep Europe safe. Even Russia's ally in the Holy Alliance, Austria-Hungary, mobilized to hold back Russian troops, as the "test" invasion had put Russian troops on either side of the Danube River, Austria-Hungary's water route to the Black Sea. Furthermore, with

Seward's Folly and Alaska

Austria-Hungary gearing up militarily, Russia's other ally, Prussia, went to a **war footing** as a preventative measure as well.

At the last minute, a conference was convened at Vienna, attended by Russia, Austria-Hungary, Prussia, the Ottomans, Britain, and France, as a means of trying to avert all-out war in Europe. Out of these negotiations came the Vienna Note, a diplomatic document proposing a compromise. Hoping to avoid war, Russia was inclined to accept. The Vienna Note said that the tsar would remove Russian troops from Moldavia and Wallachia. Additionally, as the protector of the Orthodox Church, Russia would have nominal control over Orthodox Christians living within the borders of the Ottoman Empire.

While the tsar accepted the Note's agreements and started the evacuation of the troops, which lessened tensions with Austria-Hungary and Prussia, the Ottoman sultan refused to agree and instead declared war on Russia in October 1853. The sultan wanted revenge on Russia for the invasion of Ottoman lands and had been assured by the British diplomat of British backing in any conflict that might ensue.

While British support might not seem like much given how close the Russian forces were and how thinly spread the British forces were around the globe at the time, for the Ottomans, the British forces seemed a necessity. At this time, the Russian navy had the most, and arguably best trained and equipped, sailors in the world, but the British navy had the most ships. The Russian Black Sea fleet included fifteen new ships of the line that the tsar had ordered built in the 1840s, along with the nine that existed before, and along with the British, had a larger number of steamships in its navy than other nations' fleets.

While other nations respected Russia's naval power (indeed, when Prussia tried to take control of some Danish territories, the appearance of Russian ships siding with

those of Denmark caused the conflict to end diplomatically without any Russian shots being fired), Britain saw Russia as a dangerous rival and thought this entanglement in the Middle East would help to deplete the Russian Black Sea fleet.

The Crimean War officially started on October 11, 1853 when ships of the Ottoman Navy opened fire on the steamers *Prut* and *Ordinarets*, and on eight Russian gunboats on the Danube. Eight days later, Nicholas I declared war on the Ottoman Empire. The war saw the devastating power of delayed-fuse explosive, flat-trajectory, high-velocity Paixhans guns by the Russian naval forces, and the equally devastating lack of training and communication

Seward's Folly and Alaska

The charge of the Light Brigade at Balaclava, October 15, 1854

the British military suffered from. One of these instances was immortalized in the poem "The Charge of the Light Brigade" by Alfred Lord Tennyson. It also showed the importance of new technologies such as railroads and telegraphs in modern warfare, to aid the military but also to keep the populations informed of the war's progress or lack thereof. Discontent from this fast transfer of information resulted in events like the British people expressing dissatisfaction with the defeat of the Light Brigade at Balaclava by having a "snowball riot" in Trafalgar Square; fifteen hundred people gathered to protest the war, throwing snowballs at buses, cabs, and pedestrians. The police and the military later broke up the riot.

France, which had sent far more soldiers to the war than Britain and suffered far more casualties, wanted the war to end, as did Austria. The two sides negotiated in Paris and on March 30, 1856, signed the Treaty of Paris. In compliance with Article III of the Treaty, Russia restored to the Ottoman Empire all parts of the Ottoman territory occupied by Russian troops. Russia also ceded some land in Bessarabia at the mouth of the Danube to Moldavia. In accordance with Article IV, Britain, France, Sardinia, and Turkey restored to Russia the towns and ports of

Sevastopol, Balaklava, Kamish, Eupatoria, Kerch, Jenikale, Kinburn, and all other territories the allies had captured that originally belonged to Russia. Articles XI and XIII required the tsar and the sultan to agree to demilitarize the Black Sea, which the two nations shared. This weakened Russia, as it could no longer threaten the Ottomans with a naval presence. Although Moldavia and Wallachia were technically returned to the Ottoman Empire, they more or less became independent. The Ottoman Empire won credibility from the European powers, who promised to respect its independence and integrity.

While this essentially set the borders of countries back to what they had been before the war, due to some of the additional sanctions, Russia came out the worse for it, leaving the British with a more powerful and versatile navy in the latter half of the nineteenth century. The fact that the British did not do what they had told the Russian ambassador they would before the outbreak of the war, and in fact, sided with the Ottoman so as to directly oppose Russian forces with their own army and naval forces, gave a distaste to any future Russian dealings with the British.

Not surprisingly, after these global events Russia was looking to divest itself of the Alaska Territory, but they definitely did not want to sell it to the British. That, of course, left the Americans as potential buyers, and in 1857 James Buchanan had just become the president. Buchanan was already known to the Russians, as he had been the minister to Russia from 1832 to 1833 when Andrew Jackson had been president. Now, as president himself, Buchanan might have been receptive to the Russians, but he had pressing problems of his own to deal with at home. The United States was in turmoil; the question of slavery and secession that had been put off by President Fillmore was coming to a head. Buchanan faced dealing with the Dred

Scott decision, which pushed the sentiments of the North and South farther apart, and the resulting violence between anti-slavery and pro-slavery settlers in what became known as the Bleeding Kansas crisis.

A formal offer from the United States was assessed by the Russians in 1857, and they attempted to calculate the value of the Alaska Territory. Baron Ferdinand von Wrangell, who had been chief manager (governor) of the Russian-American Company, wrote up a memorandum to the tsar detailing expected revenue and value. In it, he stated that a private Russian company buying the territory should be charged about $5.6 million, but, if the United States was to be the buyer, the cost should be $15 million, to help offset the compensation from interest on loans. They were hoping to get this settled before 1859, as that was when existing agreements with the Hudson's Bay Company would run out. However, with the American turmoil, there was no way to leverage anywhere near the $15 million. By 1861, as Abraham Lincoln became president and shots were fired at Fort Sumter in South Carolina, starting the Civil War, the Russians realized that there was no way the Americans could buy the territory.

Tsar Alexander II also had problems at home. In 1861, he emancipated the serfs, giving them land and freedom. The state bought the lands from the peasants' landowners. Alexander expected that the peasants would be motivated to produce enough crops to not only feed themselves but also sell on the international market, the taxes from which could help finance the government's expenses and debts. By 1864, the tsar was instituting reforms in the local governments and the judicial system. Larger towns actually had a court system with juries, but there weren't enough resources to extend that system to smaller villages, so a system of judicial cases being decided on their merits, not on precedent, was implemented.

Russian funds were also being used for educating the populace, relaxing censorship rules, and expanding infrastructure. To help support the Russian economy, a State Bank was founded. These reforms were to help keep the peace within the Russian populace, as those in power were worried that the system might violently fall apart. But while the United States was fighting and then repairing after its Civil War, Russia was busy with its own issues. Alaska would have to wait.

Manifest Destiny

As things in both countries got back to normal, one of the driving concepts that had helped to cause some of the turmoil in the United States was that of manifest destiny. Journalist John L. O'Sullivan was the first person to use the phrase in 1845, in an essay advocating the United States **annexation** of Texas. While this expression did not catch on in public use, his second use of the phrase in a newspaper article—addressing the disputed northern boundary of the Oregon Territory, whose northernmost boundary went as far north as the southern claim of Russian Alaska—did. He stated that the United States should claim the whole of the Oregon Territory, "And that claim is by the right of our manifest destiny to overspread and to possess the whole of the continent which Providence has given us for the development of the great experiment of liberty and federated self-government entrusted to us."

O'Sullivan had a concept of manifest destiny being a moral, **enfranchising** movement of citizens moving into territories, setting up their own governments, and of their own accord applying to join the United States. The concept was never fully defined before being accepted into common usage and ended up meaning many things to different people. Military actions, such as the provocative 1812 attack on British Canadians, have been attributed to this spirit of manifest destiny as the thought was that when the Americans attacked the British, the Canadians would rise up and fight the British, then join the United States. Likewise, during the Mexican-American War of 1846, there were calls of "All Mexico" from those who backed annexing all of Mexico when the war was over.

After the Civil War ended, the now trained and outfitted military was working to subdue and contain the Native Americans on the territories of the Great Plains, opening the way for more and more settlers. After the Great Plains and the Rocky Mountains were settled, it would close the gap between Texas and California, and Wisconsin and Oregon. As Canada and Mexico were already claimed, there was nowhere else to expand.

This was the situation, looking forward, that William H. Seward stepped into. As secretary of state for President Buchanan, he was in charge of foreign affairs. Seward was a well-seasoned politician, having served as a senator for New York State as well as two terms as governor. He was also a prominent politician, a favored presidential candidate going up against Abraham Lincoln for the Republican endorsement. After Lincoln won the presidency, he asked Seward to be his secretary of state. Seward almost declined, as he didn't think Lincoln would take his advice, but he ended up taking the post and finding that he had an important role to play in winning the Civil War. He managed to keep England from supporting the Confederates and smoothed things over when two Confederate commissioners returning from Cuba were removed from a British steamer by a Union gunboat. These incidents helped to break the Confederates. His advice to Lincoln to withhold the Emancipation Proclamation until after a Union victory served to rally the support for the war in the North.

Perhaps the greatest testament to Seward's abilities is that after Lincoln's assassination (during which Seward was stabbed in the neck as part of the plot), Andrew Johnson, who succeeded Lincoln as president, kept him on for the next term. When the war was over, Seward contemplated what the United States needed. Given the way the country had expanded over the previous half-century, he decided that what it needed was more space. In looking at the only part of North America that was not owned by the Mexicans or British Canadians, there was only Russian Alaska. Given the importance of this real estate, after the Civil War issues had pretty well calmed down in 1866, Seward began talks with Russian diplomats, inquiring about them selling Alaska, and bringing up the offer from 1857.

In December 1866, Tsar Alexander II met with his ministers in St. Petersburg and made the final decision to sell. Alexander set $5 million as the floor for his negotiators, meaning that they would not accept anything less. Accordingly, he sent the Russian ambassador to the United States, Eduard de Stoeckl, back to Washington with instructions to finalize terms for the deal with Seward. Because Seward's eagerness to purchase Alaska was well known, the Russians had the advantage in the negotiation. The final price was $7.2 million. Seward then had to go talk to President Johnson.

Some have seen Seward as manipulative in this endeavor, moving forward with negotiations before getting the go-ahead from the president. One writer, in describing him, said that, "in method he was a diplomatist of the old school, quiet, suave, secretive, aiming above all things to avoid taking the public into his confidence." But at this time his solitary diplomacy was warranted, as President Johnson had more immediate issues to deal with than foreign negotiations. The Civil War had not yet been over for a year, and the Union Army was effectively the police force for many areas of the South. Johnson was trying to navigate reconciliation of the Northern and Southern states and political figures while dealing with harsh criticism from the more radical elements of his own party, the Republicans. At the time that Seward approached Johnson, the president was in the midst of **impeachment** proceedings by the House of Representatives for not being harsh enough in his treatment of the South after the war.

Seward's talk with Johnson went well, despite having to admit that the actual cost for the land was $7 million, and that bribes made up for the rest. Only a few people were privy to that information, but it would end up being part of the uproar that would hit the media later, after the purchase had been made. The Alaska Treaty was signed in secret on March 30, 1867 (the occasion now celebrated as Seward's Day) but the purchase money was not approved by Congress until July 1868.

Obstacles to Finalizing the Purchase

This was the period when Alaska was referred to in the media as "Seward's Folly," "Seward's Icebox," and "Johnson's Polar Bear Garden." While some people did, in fact, picture Alaska as nothing but a sheet of useless ice, it seems that the majority thought that Alaska was worth acquiring. Much of what we would see as a media attack on the deal was from newspapers friendly to the "Radical Republicans" who were seeking to impeach Johnson, or at least impede any plan that he might put forward that would give him public credit. The outrage of other, more ordinary people, was not about the actual purchase itself, but rather the secrecy that Seward undertook to get to the treaty. But, if most people thought buying Alaska was a good idea, why did it take so long to get through Congress?

There were many obstacles to the **appropriation**. On the one hand, the president was undergoing impeachment; on the other, people were concerned about American **imperialism**. However, the primary objection came from the Perkinses, a wealthy Massachusetts family. The Perkinses argued that they held debt from the Russians, who had purchased weapons through the Perkinses during the Crimean War, and they expected the US to give them money from the deal to settle the debt. They worked with **lobbyists** and used political favors to hold up the process. Seward received important political support on Capitol Hill from Senator Charles Sumner of Massachusetts, chairman of the Senate Foreign Relations Committee. In April 1867, Sumner delivered a speech that helped turn the vote in favor of the agreement. Sumner's constituents consisted of New England whalers and traders, who had much to gain from access to North Pacific waters. Sumner also aligned with many Republicans, who had a general policy of removing monarchical rule from North America. Two key members, Representative Nathaniel Banks (head of the House Foreign Affairs Committee) and Representative Thaddeus Stevens (head of the Ways and Means Committee), went from supporting the Perkins claim to backing the Alaska payment as it stood. The last debates and

PREPARING FOR THE HEATED TERM.

King Andy and his man Billy lay in a great stock of Russian ice in order to cool down the Congressional majority.

A political cartoon from April 1867, lampooning Johnson and Seward, titled "Preparing for the heated term; King Andy and his man Billy lay in a great stock of Russian ice in order to cool down the Congressional majority."

Seward's Folly and Alaska

final vote were held on a summer day when the temperature in Washington, DC, was above 100 degrees Fahrenheit (37 degrees Celsius), inspiring many predictable jokes, such as commenting on how "at least there would be enough ice to cool the rest of the country." On October 18, 1867, American soldiers raised the United States flag over Sitka.

Allegations afterward claimed that the bribe money paid to the Russians was actually paid out by Stoeckl, the Russian ambassador. Money was paid to Representative Banks, lobbyist Robert J. Walker (a friend of Seward's), the editor of a powerful Washington newspaper, the "incorruptible Thaddeus Stevens," and eight other congressmen. In 1869, Congress, responding to the rumors and allegations in newspapers, launched an inquiry into these secret payments to lobbyists and journalists. Attention turned away from politicians and toward journalists, however, when an investigative reporter for the *New York Sun* named Uriah Painter exposed a lobbyist who was also a former senator from Mississippi. The lobbyist revealed to the Congressional inquiry that Painter himself had only written his exposés when his own request for a bribe was denied. Painter in turn denied the allegations, but the story set off a media firestorm that proved highly entertaining to the officials in Washington, DC. Fortunately for Congress, it also helped to draw attention away from its members, helping to conceal any evidence of their own guilt. This does show how much political work Seward had to do to get the purchase made, and all for the country's good, rather than for his own personal gain. When all was said and done, Seward paid about two cents per acre (0.4 hectare) for Alaska. When he was asked to name his greatest achievement, Seward said "The purchase of Alaska, but it will take the people a generation to find it out."

This was not the only project of this type that Seward was working on at the time. Seward also attempted to

"Baron" Eduard de Stoeckl would be a focus of Congressional hearings on the back room deals and bribes involved in the sale of the Alaska Territory.

Seward's Folly and Alaska

The actual check (Treasury Warrant) used to pay for the Alaska Territory.

purchase the Danish West Indies (Virgin Islands) and to annex the Dominican Republic in the Caribbean. Not content with having reached the Pacific Coast, Seward wanted to move into the Pacific itself, to support both trade with the East and the defense of the United States. While he successfully oversaw the annexation of Midway Island, he was not successful in gaining control of the Hawaiian Islands.

As reports of Americans settling Alaska reached Asia, Russians were crestfallen. Newspapers across the country called it nothing but a "mean, disgusting joke upon the Russian society." Many considered the sale of the land yet another failure committed by Tsar Alexander II, and the money Russia had been given only a fraction of what the land was worth. The Russian government responded that the sale of Alaska was in the best interests of the country. On the one hand, the government argued, Alaska was too far removed from Russia to be appropriately governed; on the other, it was hoped that the sale would benefit the diplomatic relationship between Russia and the United States.

Vitus Bering's expedition being wrecked
on the Aleutian Islands in 1741

CHAPTER THREE

Alaskan Explorers

The Alaska Territory was first noted by European explorers as early as 1648 when a Russian Cossack named Semen Dezhnev claimed to have rounded the cape of Asia by the point of what is now called Mys Dezhneva. This is the easternmost point of the Asian continent in the Bering Strait, less than 20 miles (32.1 km) from Alaska's coast. However, his official report was somehow mislaid and a Dutch seaman named Vitus Bering was ordered by the Russian Tsar Peter I to find where the Russian Empire met North America. In 1728, after a suitable ship was built at Petropavlosk on the Kamchatka coast and christened the *St. Gabriel*, Bering set off. He reached the strait that is now named after him but never actually encountered North America, as there was a heavy fog on the waters as he sailed up the strait and back down into the Pacific. While his course probably took him only a few miles off the coast of Alaska, he never saw it to record or explore it, and he reported no connecting lands to the north of the eastern coasts of the Russian Empire.

Bering's second **expedition** in 1741 included two ships. Bering himself sailed the *St. Peter* and his second-in-command, Aleksey Chirikov, captained the *St. Paul*. As they sailed east from Petropavlosk, the two ships got separated in a storm. Chirikov continued on to the west and sighted the coast of North America at Prince of Wales Island, near the southernmost tip of modern Alaska. Chirikov's voyage was unlucky, however, as he lost both of his shore boats and a number of men, thus rendering him unable to adequately explore the area. He then turned north and continued to **survey** the coast in a general sense, finally turning back west along the Aleutian Islands and returning to Russia.

Bering had turned his ship toward the north sooner than Chirikov did and landed on what he named Saint Elias Island (now known as Kayak Island), just 62 miles (100 km) southeast of modern-day Cordova, Alaska. Here, his crew stayed ashore only long enough to collect fresh water, but it gave a German surgeon and naturalist by the name of Georg Wilhelm Steller some time to investigate and find "signs of people and their doings," which included a still-smoldering fire, a log hollowed out to be a cooking vessel, a storage pit with items including bundles of fish, and arrowheads. While Steller was upset at not being able to stay, explore, and perhaps meet the people whose items he found, he took some items back to the ship and started the first ethnographic collection of artifacts from the Alaskan Natives. He would later complain that it took him ten years to get to the New World, and then he had only ten hours to explore it.

Bering, however, felt that he had good reason to rush. His two ships had been separated, and he and his crew were starting to show the effects of scurvy. As the *St. Peter*

A 1762 map of North America, with a highly inaccurate image of the Pacific Northwest

made its way back, charting the coastline and some of the Aleutian Islands, they encountered some of the **Aleuts** in their **kayaks**. However, as the trip went on and Bering grew too weak to command, they sought refuge on an island (now named Bering Island) only 341 miles (548 km) from the harbor at Petropavlosk. The ship was wrecked. Bering and many of his crew died on this island, but the survivors, as well as the returning crew of the *St. Paul*, all reported that the coast of Alaska was lush and rich with seals, foxes, and sea otters, all valuable for the fur trade. This information sparked more than thirty known trading ventures over the next few decades, and two official naval surveys of the Alaskan islands and coasts (Synd in 1764 and Krenitsyn and Levashev in 1768), though these were merely filed away and not made widely available. There was a map of the area, made by Jacob von Stählin in 1774, which erroneously showed Alaska as a large island and put the Aleutian Islands haphazardly in the wrong places, causing problems for future explorers and very likely early traders looking to become rich.

Other Nations Explore

The Russians were not the only explorers charting and claiming these areas. The Spanish came north from their Californian holdings to survey the coasts of what would become Oregon, Washington, British Columbia, and Alaska. In 1775, Juan Francisco de la Bodega y Quadra became the first Spaniard to reach the Alaska territory, claiming Baranof Island and Prince of Wales Island for Spain as he searched for a fabled **Northwest Passage**, reported by Bartholomew de Fonte in 1640, that would lead to Hudson's Bay on the other side of North America. The British also were interested in exploring this area, and in 1788, James Cook also went looking for a northwest passage but in a more scientific manner than relying on Fonte's descriptions. An English explorer named Samuel Hearne had, between 1771 and 1772, traveled overland to the northwest from Hudson's Bay and reported on encountering the Arctic Ocean, which had about 3 miles (4.8 km) of navigable space between the coast and the ice. Cook planned to head north along the coast of North America and swing back along the northern coast toward the east. With two ships, the *Resolution* and the *Discovery*, Cook sailed along the coast and claimed a site for England near what is now Anchorage.

Cook attempted to use von Stählin's map, but he finally discarded it in frustration as a strait between North America and the "island" of Alaska never materialized, and he was happy to chart an accurate map himself. His voyage charted the southern coastline of Alaska, the Aleutian Islands they encountered (they went out as far as Unalaska Island), and some of the area along the Bering Strait on both the North American and Asian sides. Cook was confused by how Bering could have missed North America, and at first doubted it was where Bering had been. He continued north and encountered the **ice pack** of the Arctic Ocean in August and was forced to turn back.

After Cook returned and reported the wealth of sea otters he saw, many European and United States traders set off to the area, only to find that the "coastline" mapped by Cook and the Spanish was sometimes fjords and **sounds**, and other times islands with more waterways behind them. While the Spanish and British clashed over areas farther south, they continued to search for Forte's northwest passage, and the French explorer La Péruse claimed some of what is now southern Alaska for France. It wasn't until George Vancouver's 1792–1794 British expedition charted

The flag of the Russian-American Company, used in 1806

the Pacific coast from what is now Kodiak Island down to Washington State, that both the Spanish and British were convinced that there was no northwest passage. Any travel from the Pacific to the Atlantic in North America would have to be an overland route.

Most of these voyages dealt with the coasts, but there is much more to Alaska than its coasts. There were some excursions into the interior, and up until the 1820s, the explorations were dominated by Russians and Russian interests. The first recorded explorer of the interior was a hunter named Vasily Ivanov, who was employed by the Lebedev-Lastochkin Company during the 1790s to explore along the upper Kuskokwim River. This was not, however, seen by many as useful, as trading along the coast by ship was much more profitable.

By 1799, the Russian-American Company was created by the tsar's charter to bring together a number of competing Russian trading firms and create a monopoly over the resources of Russia, to combat the higher prices American and British traders were willing to pay the Natives of Alaska for their furs and goods. One of the outcomes of this, is that the fur supply on the coasts became more depleted. In order to keep up with Russian and European demands, the traders had to move farther inland to areas that were still rich in the animals that provided furs. One of the resources that the Russian-American Company found and used was the Native Aleuts, many of whom were enslaved or pressed into service to aid the company.

There were a number of trading outposts that sprang up as traders and Aleuts worked to get what the other had. One had been on Unalaska Island since the 1770s and was known as Captain's Harbor. The first permanent settlement was Three Saints Harbor, which was founded in 1783 by the Shelikhov-Golikov Company, then moved in 1792 to St. Paul's Harbor, where it would stay to become the modern-day city of Kodiak, on Kodiak Island. In 1799, a settlement was founded at Kenai, just southwest of modern Anchorage.

Exploring Inland

As the explorers ventured inland, waterways often helped them. In 1816, Otto von Kotzebue, a Russian naval officer and **navigator**, led an expedition to chart more of the western coast of Alaska, discovering the Kotzebue Sound and spending time there so that naturalists and artists could explore and record the area. In 1818, Petr Koraskovsky and other members of his expedition left Kodiak and crossed the Alaskan Peninsula and explored the Nushagak Bay area. Off to the east of that, Afansy Klimovsky explored up the Copper River. One of Koraskovsky's men, Fedor Kolmakov, would return to the area in 1819 to set up a trading post on the Bay called New Aleksandr Redoubt.

Still, the Russians weren't the only ones exploring in the area. In 1825, British naval officer Frederick Beechey was tasked with sailing through the Bering Strait in an attempt to meet up with another British naval officer, John Franklin, who was attempting his second overland expedition to try and discover a northwest passage. The two would never meet, but in 1826, they would come close. Franklin and his expedition followed the Mackenzie River in Canada to the Arctic Coast and headed west, while Beechey sailed north along the coast of Russian Alaska to about Point Hope, where he noted a very large village of Natives. Franklin's party covered over 329 miles (530 km) of coast but was forced to turn back by extremely cold weather. While the same cold stopped the progress of Beechey's ship at Icy Cape, he had brought a schooner-rigged barge. He sent Thomas Elson off in it to try sailing in the waters the ship couldn't make it through. Elson made it to Cape Barrow, the land farthest north in Alaska, just past the modern city of Barrow, before he was forced back. The two groups had surveyed to within 146 miles (235 km) of each other. That final length wouldn't be surveyed until 1837 when Peter Dease and Thomas Simpson of the Hudson's Bay Company would close the gap.

Many of the nautical-based explorers had, or were, navigators who knew how to take bearings and make more accurate maps, but land explorers often didn't use these skills. So to aid in the exploration of the interior, the Russian-American Company sent a number of Russian **creoles** to study at St. Petersburg's Kronstadt Navigation College during the 1820s and 1830s. They came back to Alaska with more of the skills that would be needed for more precise exploration, which raised the expectations for other explorers as well.

One Russian creole named Semyon Lukin explored with Ivan Vasiliev in 1829–1830 along the waterways north and northeast of New Aleksander Redoubt, heading far up into the Kuskokwim **drainage** and following the river back down to the coast. In 1832, Lukin and Kolmakov would travel back to that area and set up a trading post called Kolmakov's Redoubt. In 1833, the Russian-American Company would build a trading base called St. Michael's on Norton Sound, just to the west of the mouth of the Yukon River, which would turn out to lead deep into the interior. Lukin and Andrei Galazunov—another Russian creole—explored the Yukon River in 1833, and in 1834 they made it overland from St. Michael's to Kolmakov's Redoubt. Galazunov tried to continue overland from there down to Cook's Inlet, but he turned back due to the cold and lack of supplies.

In 1838, another of the Russian creoles, Petr Malakhov, made his way from St. Michael's to the Yukon River and then to the confluence of the Koyukuk River. He returned the next year to set up a small Russian military outpost with a single, fortified building called a blockhouse at Nulato, just 15 miles (25 km) downstream of the confluence.

It was not just the Natives who the Russians may have feared in setting up a military outpost. The British, in the form of the Hudson's Bay Company, were coming overland through Canada and into the Alaskan area. In 1840, Robert Campbell, a Hudson's Bay Company agent, made his way down the Pelly River, which runs into the Yukon River. John Bell, another agent, opened Peel's River Post on the Mackenzie River in Canada (later renamed Fort McPherson), then continued to explore west, making his way over to and then down the Porcupine River to its confluence with the Yukon River. There, in 1847, Fort Yukon would be established as a Hudson's Bay Company trading post.

While the Russians continued to explore, the pace of their explorations slowed, but some yielded more than just maps. In 1842–1844, Lavrentiy Zagoskin led an expedition that investigated the Yukon, Kuskokwim, and Innoko River drainages. During this time, he interacted with Native Athapaskans and Eskimos and documented

RUSSIAN BLOCK HOUSE
SITKA

their ways of life in the interior, adding to what was already known about the lives of those inhabiting coastal communities. In 1848, Petr Doroshin, a geologist, reported finding gold in a stream that ran into Kenai Bay. While this would bring a few prospectors who felt that the California gold fields were too crowded, Native massacres in 1848 on the Copper River and in 1851 at the Nulato outpost would slow official explorations even more.

A typical octagonal Russian blockhouse in Sitka, Alaska

Seward's Folly and Alaska

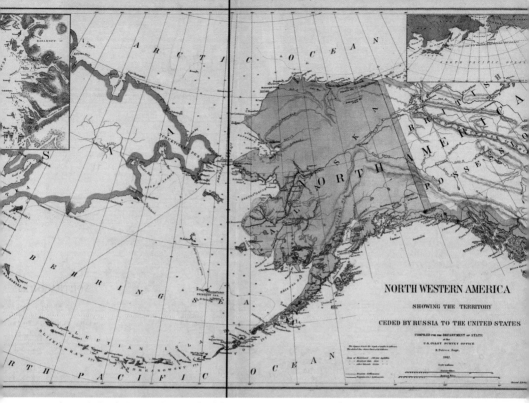

The red-shaded area shows all of the Alaskan lands ceded to the United States in 1867.

American Exploration

Even before the United States owned the Alaska Territory, they had been surveying there for business purposes. In 1865, Western Union Telegraph was looking for a way to link North America to Europe, and the Bering Strait seemed an easier way to get there than laying cable across the Atlantic Ocean. The plan called for survey teams to scout along the Yukon River up to Fort Yukon and then proceed east to meet up with a Canadian survey team. While the survey was slowed by one of the leaders (Robert Kennicott) dying along the way, the Americans continued and collected ethnographic and natural historic items as they learned about the Alaskan country. However, even for the survey team, news didn't travel quickly in Alaska. William Healey Dall was the first team member to find out that they were actually in the United States and not Russian territory on February 3, 1868.

In order to combat the power of the Hudson's Bay Company in the northwest of North America, the Alaska Commercial Company was set up. In 1869, Charles Raymond took a steam-powered paddlewheel ship up the Yukon River to Fort Yukon and determined that the trading post was within the United States' Alaskan territory. However, the government initially paid the most attention to the coast, with extensive Army and Treasury surveys occurring there over the 1870s.

Starting with Henry Ray's 1879 long-term scientific mission to study the weather in Uglamie, and John Muir's account of Glacier Bay, this began to change. In 1883, the United States Army sent Frederick Schwatka on an expedition from Fort William H. Seward. He traveled through the Chilkoot Pass, after which he built a raft at Lake Lindeman and ran rapids and floated down the Yukon River until he encountered an Alaska Commercial Company steamship, which he boarded and took all the way to St. Michael. His accounts, both written and oral, served to stir up the American populace as to the beauty and possibility of this new land. During the same year, the Navy dispatched George M. Stoney and John Cantwell to explore along the Kobuk River. The Army sent Henry T. Allen on an expedition in 1885 to survey the Copper River drainage, the earlier Russian attempt at such an expedition having ended in massacre. Allen explored three huge river drainages, not just the Copper but also those of the Tanana and the Koyukuk Rivers. The next year, Stoney made an overland exploration from Point Barrow to Nulato. During the 1890s more systematic surveys were undertaken as US

Glacier Bay in 1899, much the same as the view John Muir romanticized in 1879. It would become one of the early tourist destinations for excursions into Alaska.

Geological Survey teams moved throughout the territory, not only finding the height of mountain ranges but accurately placing them and their passes on maps.

When gold was discovered in smaller strikes in 1861, 1872, and larger ones in 1880, 1886, and then on from 1888 to 1909, the gold rushes over the subsequent years brought thousands of prospectors, businessmen, and settlers deeper into Alaska's interior. They began to explore their surroundings in much more detail. Through these, much of Alaska's beauty and natural resources were discovered.

The interior of a Native home on
Norton Sound, from the 1860s

CHAPTER FOUR

Settling Alaska

The first people in Alaska probably arrived during the Wisconsin Ice Age (approximately 85,000 to 11,000 years ago) when water from the seas was taken up in snow and glaciers on land that didn't melt due to the cold weather. This lowered the sea levels and allowed the seabed between Alaska and Siberia to become dry land and scrub tundra, populated by trees such as spruce, birch, willow, and alder. At its maximum, about 21,000 years ago, the land bridge spanned around 1,000 miles (1,600 km) from north to south. The first land connections occurred about 43,000 years ago and were reclaimed by the rising seawaters again around 11,000 years ago, but the wide-open territory was home to humans for easily 10,000 years (the area stayed free of snow due to the weather patterns coming from the Asian continent).

Alaskan Natives demonstrating their kayak skills around 1900.

These first people were Asians who had learned how to survive as big game hunters in the Northern Siberian steppes and who had moved into the Beringian Land Bridge area following their prey. As much as these peoples were nomadic, those who did not travel by boat farther down the coasts into North America were stopped as they came up against the glaciers that had built up in the Alaska and Brooks moutanin ranges. As the sea levels rose, the land bridge, over several thousand years, shrank until it finally was severed as the waters of the Arctic Ocean met those of the Pacific. The people trapped on the eastern side of this divide were slowly forced farther east into present-day Alaska. There is firm archaeological evidence of them living there by fifteen thousand years ago, though they could have reasonably been there since before twenty-five thousand years ago. These people wore relatively tight-fitting clothing made from the skins and furs of the animals they hunted, sewn with bone needles and sinew. Many of their tools were made of bone, and artifacts indicate that they hunted elk, horse, and caribou. While many of these early peoples would migrate south as the ice melted, some stayed and mixed with the next immigrants who arrived from Asia by boat.

These next peoples traveled across the disappearing tail of the land bridge and then the narrow Bering Strait

waters some nine thousand to fourteen thousand years ago. They were the ancestors of the Tlingit, Eyak, and Athabaskan Native Americans of modern Alaska. These peoples would move along the rivers and into the interior of Alaska as the land thawed, and marine resources in rivers and lakes took over what had been frozen tundra. Many of the nomadic Athabaskan groups would follow seasonal patterns of living, hunting migrating caribou in the fall, catching the spawning salmon in the spring, and hunting and trapping as seasons and environments allowed.

After these people came another wave of peoples from Asia who came by boat between four thousand and ten thousand years ago. These people likely followed the

Aleutian Island archipelago or came across the Bering Strait, and they mostly remained along the coastal areas. There, they collected shellfish and coastal plants and hunted larger marine mammals like seals and sea otters. Some groups even hunted whales. These groups would become the Aleuts and the Inuit Natives in modern Alaska.

The Russians Settle

The next group of people to move in were Russians, who set up trading outposts to use the hunting skills of the Native Alaskans to cash in on the fur trade. Because this trade involved sea-going ships taking furs to Asia so they could return with trade goods, and the hunters collecting the furs often traveled by kayak, most of these early sites were on islands, or in sheltered bays. Many of these sites were also chosen for military security, more against the Native populations than against other European explorers.

Military outposts (forts) usually consisted of log buildings protected by stockade walls built with upright posts. A fort might included one or two defensive watchtowers called blockhouses, apartments for officials, barracks, storerooms, and special buildings such as blacksmith shops or Russian Orthodox churches or chapels. While many of these were seasonal or lasted only for a few years, some of them not only survived but thrived, becoming cities like Kodiak, Seward, and Juneau. During these early times, the only people there were the traders, explorers, military personnel, administrators, sailors, possibly clergy, and specialist workers (like blacksmiths), unless the settlement was near some useful resource like lumber or coal which could be extracted and shipped back to Asia for a profit. In those cases, laborers would also be at the settlement to harvest the resource, and in the case of lumber (like at the settlement of Resurrection Bay, which would become Seward), sometimes instead of shipping the wood back, it was made directly into ships.

However, these settlers seldom had long-term goals of staying. Their plans involved making a fortune, or a good living, in the Alaska Territory and then returning to their homelands. Perhaps one of the reasons for this mindset was the hostility of the Native populations. In the late 1700s and early 1800s the mistreatment of the Natives by the Russians had caused several uprisings and attacks on trading posts and military outposts, which the Russian military forces dealt with harshly. Alexander Baranov had been sent to Alaska in 1792 by the Shelikhov-Golikov Company to manage the trading, and his expansion of the trade angered Tlingit and Yakut Natives along the southern coast of Alaska. This made the area more dangerous for not only the Russians but also for non-local Natives working for the Russians, such as the Aleuts.

One can see a reflection of this troubled time in the number of Russians in Alaska at different points in time. Data from 1788 indicates that the various Russian companies involved in the fur trade had between 450 and 500 people in the whole of the Alaska Territory. As the fur trade declined and the troubles with the Natives increased, the number of Russians in Alaska dropped to 225 by 1799—but that didn't mean that the Russians were abandoning Alaska. In fact, the town of Sitka, which had been the site of a massacre of the Russians and Aleuts by the local Tlingit tribe in 1802, was retaken and fortified by the Russians under Baranov in 1804. Baranov's forces fought tough battles to exterminate and drive the Tlingit away and settled a major military force in the fortifications. By 1817, when there were again somewhere between 450 and 500 Russians in Alaska, 190 of them resided in Sitka (along with another 430 creoles and Aleuts), which was rapidly becoming the capital of the Russian administration of the territory.

This tense situation along the southern coasts helped to push more exploration and outposts into the interior of Alaska and drew in more permanent settlers. Ikogmiut, on the Yukon River, had been a fur trading outpost from 1836 to 1839, but the trading operations shifted to a different point and left the buildings deserted. In 1845, the Russian Orthodox Church made it into a mission station for the local Natives. Around the same time, at Ninilchik (and later Seldovia, Kasilof, and Knik), a "retirement village" was established, where it was proposed that employees of the trading companies who did not want to return to Russia could stay and support the trading company's endeavors in the fur trade by farming some of the rich soils and selling the food to the company directly. Yet another of the outposts became more settled near Port Graham, where in the 1850s, coal miners started to settle more permanently, and the economy of the area moved away from fur trading.

They Come for Gold, Farmland, and Oil

There were some more solitary settlers in the form of gold prospectors, after 1850 and 1861 reports of gold pebbles in the Russian River and Telegraph Creek drainages got out. The influx of prospectors and miners, small as it was compared to later gold rushes, caused the Russian government officials in Alaska to worry about whether they could maintain control with so many non-Russians entering the territory, giving yet another reason why Russia wanted to sell Alaska. This was compounded by the fact that these finds were small, and many thought they would not give profitable returns.

Prospectors making their way to the Chilcoot Pass in 1898, bound for the Klondike gold fields on the other side of the mountains.

The first paying **gold strikes** in Alaska were in Windham Bay, just south of the town of Sumdum (now the Endicott Arm area), and at Powers Creek, at the base of the Sumdum Glacier. It was 1869, and Alaska had been under United States control for two years. This gold strike heralded the beginning of the gold rushes that would draw thousands of miners northward, through the Klondike trails into the gold-rich Yukon. Cities like Juneau and Skagway were populated with prospectors hoping to strike it rich.

With the gold miners came the metal assessors and gold purchasers, and the merchants, setting up general stores or dealing in special luxury goods for rich miners, tavern and saloon-keepers, brewers, launderers, post office workers, blacksmiths, porters, criminals, and eventually lawmen. Some of these boomtowns turned into modern towns and cities with other means of survival, while others (like Sumdum mentioned above) slowly died away as the gold veins petered out and profitability lessened.

Farmers arrived as well, despite the short growing season that limited what plants could be grown. The thought of gain for these agriculturists was that the extremely long (in total) daylight hours would make up for the limited choices of crops. While most of these settlers ended up staying in the Matanuska Valley, the Kenai Peninsula, or the Tanana Valley, **homesteaders** tried to farm in many areas.

The Homestead Act, enacted in 1862, gave people the chance to own their own piece of 160 acres (64.7 ha) of land in one of the western states or territories. All a person had to do was build a house and farm a piece of land for five years. At the end of five years, that person would rightfully own whatever parcel of land they had claimed for himself. While the Alaska Territory wasn't purchased until 1867, and should have been covered under this Act, it was not until 1898 that Congress applied the benefits of the Homestead Act to land in Alaska. However, people traveled to Alaska slowly. The soil proved subpar for farming, travel north was expensive, and farming tools were not readily available in Alaska at that time. By 1914 less than two hundred homestead applications had been filed in Alaska. A surge in Alaskan homestead applications

A farm in southeastern Alaska, where small fruits and vegetables could grow to twice their average size, circa 1915

did come after both World War II and the Vietnam War. While some aspects of transportation and supply had improved, much of the life, work, and dealing with the weather for a homesteader hadn't changed since the 1800s. In 1976, Congress repealed the Homestead Act for most states; Alaska was the exception, where homesteaders could still claim their own slice of the state until 1986.

Most of the modern settlers in Alaska came because of the petroleum wealth. After the 1960s, petroleum became a big business in Alaska. Thousands of trained workers were needed, and even more untrained laborers to help support the drilling rigs and wells, and transport the oil.

A light tank maneuvering in a mountain pass in Alaska was just part of the WWII military presence established there in the summer of 1942.

CHAPTER FIVE

Seward's Success

For many years after the United States gained ownership of the Alaska Territory, it languished almost forgotten by the government as the settlement of the Midwest and Great Plains took precedence. This is most easily seen in the fact that for nearly twenty years after 1867 there was no civil government in the area, and almost fifty years passed before there was an official Territorial government tied to the federal government in Washington, DC.

Alaskan Gold

Three years into American control, the first of several big gold strikes occurred. Where the Russian estimates of the amount of gold in Alaska had determined that gold **mining** would not be a profitable business venture, these early strikes at Sumdum would remain profitable until World War II. Even bigger strikes near Sitka (1871), Juneau (1880), Fortymile River (1886), Nome (1898–1899), Fairbanks (1902), and Iditarod and Flat (1909) would create an industry that would be what Alaska was known for through the 1930s and 1940s. Some areas, like Fairbanks, still have working gold mines today, and several of those closed during World War II still have gold in them, though the cost to refurbish and restart the mines is too high to make them viable at today's prices.

Over the time period from 1880 to 2012, 44.4 million troy ounces (1,380 t) of gold were mined; current rates are about 26,000 troy ounces (809 kilograms) of gold per year. Additionally, more gold is panned out of streams and rivers, but some of that escapes being counted toward the total amount.

More profitable than gold, however, are Alaska's **fisheries**. The first cannery in Alaska opened in 1878 in Klawock. During the 1890s, the fishing industry produced millions of cases of canned salmon annually. When a small tax was excised on every case of salmon packaged in Alaska, the revenues contributed 70 percent to the state's overall income. The importance of Alaska's fisheries continues today. However, Alaska's salmon fisheries face stiff competition from farmed salmon. Inexpensive aquaculture, or the raising of aquatic animals for food, in Chile, Norway, and British Columbia has taken a bite out of the market for wild-caught Alaskan salmon, which is more expensive. Nevertheless, commercial fishing still makes up about 5 percent of Alaska's economic base.

Alaskan Oil

An important modern resource in Alaska that was overlooked in Seward's day is petroleum. Before the advent of drilling for petroleum, Native Americans and Europeans alike collected crude oil from naturally occurring wellsprings. In 1859, Edwin Drake discovered that drilling could yield higher outputs of crude oil and established the first oil well in Titusville, Pennsylvania. The search for oil spread to Alaska forty years later. In 1898, the first Alaskan wells were drilled on the Iniskin Peninsula. Here, oil drillers found oil mixed with seawater, but the amount of oil was so small that it could not sustain a full-blown operation. Around the same time, another group funded some drilling at Dry Bay, but these wells, along with other sites at Puale Bay at the end of the Alaskan Peninsula, were unproductive.

Oil miners eventually drilled a productive well at Katalla, located on the Gulf of Alaska, south of the Copper River delta. In 1900, investors hired a petroleum expert to examine the area. While some wells found oil in profitable quantities, the conditions were rough for the workers and expensive to supply, and finally the investors decided to quit.

By 1911, a few wells in the area had begun to produce a considerable amount of oil. However, the amount was still too low to make it worth it to ship the oil. Most of this oil was processed at a a local refinery. This meager production continued until a fire destroyed the refinery in 1933. Without the processing facility, whose cost savings were the only thing making the operation profitable, the well was abandoned.

From 1946–1954, the US Geological Survey and the navy drilled thirty-six test wells near the village of Barrow but found only two minor oil deposits. None of the oil was used, save for a small amount of natural gas that was pumped to the village for local use. It still looked as though the petroleum reserves of Alaska would be of little value outside.

It was not until the discovery of the large Swanson River **oil field** on the Kenai Peninsula in 1957 that potential oil investors became interested. While all the major American oil companies were intrigued, it was the Richfield Oil

The Prudhoe Bay Oil Field, seen here in 1971, is the largest in North America.

Company of California that was the first to invest and drill, striking oil with their very first well. The discovery was reported on July 15, 1957. The well was estimated to produce 900 barrels per day, making it the first commercially viable oil deposit in Alaska. Other companies followed the Richfield Oil Company and headed north to drill their own wells. In 1959, natural gas was discovered near the Swanson River oil field.

After Alaska was granted statehood in 1959, oil companies turned their attention to Cook Inlet. In 1962, the Middle Ground Shoal oil field was discovered off Port

Nikiski, and oil production began there in 1967. The Middle Ground shoal is considered a moderate-sized deposit. Since its discovery, nearly 1.3 billion barrels of oil and 5 trillion cubic feet (141.6 billion cubic meters) of natural gas have been extracted from Cook Inlet. At this point, the United States was no longer the world's leading oil producer, a title it had held since the 1950s when oil reserves were discovered in the Gulf of Mexico. In fact, the United States could no longer provide enough oil even for itself, as the country's need outpaced domestic production. To make up for the deficit, the US allied itself with Saudi Arabia and other Middle Eastern countries that had found their own productive oil fields. In 1967, however, another Alaskan oil deposit, this one located off Prudhoe Bay, helped reduce American reliance on foreign oil. It was this and other Alaskan deposits that helped ease America's struggles during the oil embargo in the mid-1970s.

Alaska became the center of attention in 1974 when large amounts of money started flowing to the state to finance a trans-Alaska oil pipeline to connect the Prudhoe Bay field. The 800-mile (1,287 km) pipeline took two years to complete, employed over twenty thousand workers, and cost $8 billion. Since then, many smaller fields have been connected to the pipeline, adding to Alaska's North Slope production. In 1988, this production peaked, as the fields produced 2.1 million barrels of oil each. The fields produce roughly 20 percent of the United States' domestic oil. In 1994, a law prohibiting the export of Alaskan oil was lifted, opening the state up to the world market. This brought more profit to an industry whose jobs make up just over a third of all jobs in Alaska.

Another place where Alaska has been important to the nation's economy is in tourism. Starting off with John Muir in 1879 marveling at the beauty of Alaska's glaciers,

Alaska became a tourist destination. Alaska has many geological attractions, like Denali, Glacier Bay, fjords, rivers, and the tundra, each with their own flora, fauna, and distinct ecosystems. There are also historical interests in the remnants of the Russian culture, the Native American cultures, and the cultures that sprang up from fur traders/trappers and gold rushes. In the early 1900s, steamship lines and even ferries for automobiles were in place between the southern Alaskan towns and places like Seattle, Washington, and San Francisco, California. In the 2013–2014 tourist season, more than 1.93 million tourists visited Alaska, having an economic impact of $3.9 billion, showing how valuable a business it is. For Alaska, this industry brought in $174 million in tax revenue and supported forty-six thousand jobs during the peak of the tourist season.

From the 1870s until the 1890s, the idea continually resurfaced that Alaska (or at least some of the islands along the Alaskan coast) should serve as an American **penal colony**. The Russians had had a penal colony on Chirikof Island where murderers, arsonists, and others found guilty of capital offenses were left to their own devices, living mostly on mosses, lichens, and marmots. A large number of failed prospectors and agents from the 1867 gold rush returned in 1870 with stories of how harsh the area was. Military personnel under General Charles Halleck put forth that duty in Alaska was difficult and wild, and it became a place for military prisoners to be sent so that they could easily be kept from escaping, and used as prison labor. This was based on French, Chilean, Russian, and English programs which used places such as Botany Bay, New South Wales, Siberia, or South Pacific holdings as penal colonies.

In 1870, the idea of using Vancouver Island as an American penal colony had been discussed, and the then-modern ideas of hereditary criminals supported the idea of transporting whole families to live in such a colony. In 1874, the Upper House of California put forth an official proposal to have an Alaskan prison colony created for Californian prisoners to be sent to. In 1885, the United States Senate heard a joint resolution from New Jersey Senator John Rhoderic McPherson, on behalf of his state legislature, suggesting that a portion of Alaska be used for "sequestration of dangerous criminals." In 1890, Robert Ingersoll spoke to the New York Bar Association about instituting separate island penal colonies for male and female repeat offenders, and this was taken up by an editor of the *Washington Post* who romanticized about "reform colonies" along Alaska's southeast coast. However, these things never came to be, first because of the costs, second because of the Alaskan resistance to such an idea, and third because by the 1880s, Alaska's economy was becoming bigger and more profitable.

Alaska's Military Importance

Alaska has also played a part in US military endeavors, most notably during the Cold War with the Soviet Union during the latter half of the twentieth century, but also in World War II. In 1939, Congress established a defense triangle from Panama to Hawaii to Alaska to protect America's Pacific coast. Alaska was the largest and least protected, and soon saw the construction of naval bases at Sitka, Dutch Harbor, and Kodiak. While these were unfinished by December 7, 1941, work on these bases picked up. Six months after the bombing of Pearl Harbor, the Japanese bombed the Dutch Harbor on Unalaska Island and occupied the islands of Attu and Kiska. While this Japanese invasion was merely a diversion intended to draw US ships from their base on

Midway Island to make that island an easier target, the United States could not risk abandoning the Aleutian Island Chain to the Japanese and thereby give them a route to invade the rest of North America. The Japanese used their occupation of Alaska as a source of propaganda.

The United States was in a tricky situation. Planes taking off from Kodiak and Dutch Harbor did not possess the range to attack the Japanese at Attu and Kiska, so the United States built bases on other islands that would allow them to attack further west along the Aleutians. Both pilots and ground troops soon realized they were waging war against not only the Japanese but also the weather. The weather along the 1,200-mile (1931 km) island chain is some of the worst in the world. Dense fog patches that could cut off air support or make amphibious troop landings treacherous, violent seas capable of swamping or capsizing a ship, and fierce wind storms called "williwaws" are just a few of the dangerous weather patterns common to the area. While contact with the Japanese was infrequent and generally brief for soldiers in the Aleutian Islands, the weather was frequently the more serious threat.

The battles fought in Alaska between the United States and Japan had a large impact on the lives of everyday Alaskans. Simply finding the enemy proved a struggle, as many aircraft lacked appropriate navigational or radio equipment. Planes often crashed into mountains, the sea, or each other. Native Alaskans joined the fight. They were often placed in the Alaska Scouts or the Territorial Guard, whose job it was to patrol the coasts and gather intelligence on the enemy.

The war brought with it droves of military personnel, many of whom were stationed in Alaska's smallest communities. The US government led a concentrated effort to bolster and expand the state's transportation and communication infrastructures. Alaska was suddenly abuzz with soldiers, engineers, and laborers. The 1942 Lend-Lease Program between Russia and the United States saw military planes flying over Alaska to be routed west to Russia. To account for the increase in air traffic, new airfields were built throughout Canada and Alaska to connect the northern wilderness to Fairbanks. There, the planes were transferred to Russian pilots, who would take the planes to the front lines. Up to this time, passengers and freight arrived in Alaska only two ways, either by boat or by plane. The US and Canada cooperated to build the Alaska-Canada Military Highway, a 1,420-mile (2,285 km) wilderness road that ran under the same route taken by Lend-Lease pilots. This construction boom also brought telephone lines, new oil pipelines, railways, and roughly three hundred military installations to Alaska. As the fighting in the Aleutians drew to a close, many of these facilities were closed. Although fighting in the Pacific and in Europe would continue for another two years, there would be no more Japanese attacks on Alaskan soil for the rest of the war.

Alaska on the Forefront of the Cold War

After World War II, the alliance between the Soviet Union and the United States quickly deteriorated into a period of military stalemate, underpinned by the constant threat of nuclear war that lasted nearly fifty years. From 1946 to 1991, the arms race between the United States and the Soviet Union saw an explosion in the production of nuclear weapons that were more powerful than the bombs used in World War II, balanced by a concept of "mutually assured destruction." This concept worked by deterring one side from attacking by knowing that the other side's definite retaliation would result in the destruction of the attacker, just as the nuclear attack would destroy the retaliator.

Alaska was on the frontlines on this Cold War. Its position in the Arctic Circle situated it at the shortest distance between the US and the Soviet Union. United States military planners recognized this strategic location and built hundreds of installations designed to defend the country against Soviet nuclear bombers and, later, missiles armed with nuclear warheads. The constant change in technology was driven by the frantic race to develop more powerful weapons than the other side. The defenses against those arms were demonstrated in Alaska. However, the arms race had reached such a fever pitch and weapons technology was advancing so quickly that many partially constructed defenses were scrapped, obsolete before they were finished.

This military construction drastically changed the face of Alaska during the Cold War years. Throughout the 1950s, the expansion of already existing bases, the construction of new bases, and a vast transportation, energy, and communication infrastructure to connect them occurred at a very rapid pace. This was kicked into action on August 29, 1949, when the Soviet Union shocked the world by detonating its first **atomic bomb** at a test site in Kazakhstan. It had been widely believed that the Soviets could not have a working atomic bomb until 1953. Only two months after the Soviet test, Congress authorized funding for construction of the Aircraft Control and Warning (AC&W) System, which was designed to detect Soviet bombers that could carry such a bomb and dispatch United States Air Force fighters to intercept them. Given the range of bombers at the time, it was expected that these would have to fly through Siberia or across the North Pole to reach American targets.

A Distant Early Warning (DEW) Line station in Alaska

From 1951 to 1958, eighteen AC&W stations were constructed all across Alaska. In June 1950, Soviet-supported North Korea invaded United States-supported South Korea, heightening concern about a potential Soviet attack on the United States. Tensions grew, and by 1952, it had been recognized that the AC&W system was inefficient and could not give enough advance warning of an attack, so the construction of the improved technologies of the Distant Early Warning (DEW) system facilities began between 1954 and 1959. Twenty-four DEW stations were constructed in a line across northern Alaska and along the Aleutian Islands.

In addition to these improved detection and communication capabilities, Alaska's existing Air Force bases were expanded and improved to accommodate new and better aircraft, and to carry out different missions than they had before. At its height in 1957, the Air Force presence in Alaska was made up of two hundred fighter aircraft in eight squadrons especially targeted toward the Soviet threat. Ladd Air Force Base, near Fairbanks, and Elmendorf Air Force Base, near Anchorage, comprised the northern and southern hubs of Alaska's air defense operations. These aircraft were not simply an idle force in this ideological war. Fighter aircraft in Alaska intercepted more than three hundred Soviet bombers off Alaska's coasts during the Cold War.

However, beefing up the Air Force was not the only way that the United States prepared for this war with the Soviets. Fearing a conventional military Russian invasion and occupation of Alaska in the early Cold War years, the United States turned to fishermen, bush pilots, trappers, and other private citizens with first-hand knowledge of their state for help. Alaskans were recruited to help feed intelligence to the military, newly declassified Air Force, and the FBI. The

FBI worried that an airborne invasion involving bombing and the dropping of paratroopers in the likely Alaskan targets of Nome, Fairbanks, Anchorage, and Seward was imminent. FBI director J. Edgar Hoover teamed up on a highly classified project code-named "Washtub" with the newly created Air Force Office of Special Investigations. The secret plan was to have specially trained citizens placed in key locations in Alaska, ready to hide from the invaders using hidden survival caches of food, cold-weather gear, message-coding material, and radios. While hiding, they would transmit word of enemy movements to United States forces, giving operational intelligence to aid strikes against the occupying Soviets. The program operated from 1951 to 1959, the Air Force Office of Special Investigations trained eighty-nine "stay-behind agents," and the survival caches served peacetime purposes after the threat of Soviet invasion had passed. These stay-behind agents were seen as a military necessity. There was also a parallel effort to create a standby pool of civilian operatives trained to secretly arrange for the evacuation of downed military air crews. If these crews crashed, they would be in danger of being captured by Soviet forces, who would interrogate them and learn information that could harm the United States. This evasion and escape plan was to be coordinated with the CIA's agents, who would assist with the escapes of the rescued air crews.

Alaska Becomes the Forty-Ninth State

Despite the obvious military importance of Alaska to the United States, it did not attain statehood until 1959, ninety-two years after it was acquired. It was 1916 when James Wickersham, an Alaskan delegate to Congress, introduced Alaska's first statehood bill, which failed mostly due to lack of interest on the part of Alaskans. Not even President Harding's 1923 visit to the territory could generate enough interest in statehood. There were some people who actually had a vested interest in keeping Alaska from becoming a state, not just at this point but even later. For instance, the US Maritime Act of 1920 required all commercial ships traveling between American ports be American-owned and American-built. This meant that all merchandise entering or leaving Alaska had to be transported by American ships, which, in, turn meant that all shipping had to go through Seattle. The Supreme Court reasoned that the Constitution's provision that one state should not hold sway over the commerce of another did not apply to Alaska, because Alaska was not officially a state. Routing ships through the Canadian ports of Vancouver and Prince Rupert would have saved Alaskans a lot of money. However, the Jones Act gave Seattle businesses license to charge more for their shipping services, making the cost of living in Alaska higher than it needed to be.

Attempts were made again right after World War II in 1946 but were opposed by the Republican majority in the House of Representatives, as they were afraid that a newly annexed Alaskan state would be Democratic and change the balance of power. This struggle held off any vote on Alaskan statehood until 1950, when the Korean War started, and pushed the Alaskan issue to a much lower priority for a few years. In his 1954 State of the Union address, President Eisenhower asked Congress to draft a resolution to accept Hawaii as the forty-ninth state but made no mention of Alaska joining the Union. It was clear to Eisenhower, a Republican, that Hawaii would enter the Union as a Republican state, and Alaska, meanwhile, would be Democratic. To bridge this divide, the Senate drafted a bill that would first allow Hawaii to join the Union followed by Alaska. The bill quickly became the object of fury for both parties.

An Alaskan popular publicity movement nicknamed "Operation Statehood," which was made up of prominent and influential Alaskans, put increased pressure on Congress and the president for Alaska statehood. The group argued that partisan politics stood in the way of their statehood. At one point, they even confronted President Eisenhower in the Oval Office during a meeting. Eisenhower denied allegations that partisan bickering was at the heart of the issue, pointing to the many other problems of statehood that needed addressing. As the issue was forced, a new effort to stop the statehood cause came as a Senate proposal to make Alaska and Hawaii commonwealths of the United States, with elective governorships. National columnists favored this step in newspapers across the United States, but Alaskans refused to be deterred from seeking statehood. Paying for federal taxes while being denied national representation was unfair, and many agreed that their situation very nearly resembled that of the original thirteen colonies under British rule.

As time wore on, the partisan conflicts that had stood in the way of Alaskan statehood started to waver, and the more-vocal politicans grew quieter. When Congress reconvened in January, 1958, President Eisenhower lent his full support to Alaskan statehood. While Senator Lyndon B. Johnson assured one of the biggest lobbyists for statehood that the southern senators would not filibuster the Alaska bill, there were some obstacles. Representative Thomas Pelly of Washington drafted an amendment that would retain Alaska's fish and wildlife resources under federal jurisdiction. Had this amendment passed, Pelly's constituents would be permitted to exploit Alaska's resources the same as Alaskans.

The Alaskan state flag features Polaris, the North Star.

The *Fairbanks Daily News-Miner* responded to Pelly's arrogance by printing excerpts from Edna Ferber's novel *Ice Palace*, which was set in Alaska (Ferber was an American novelist well known for her book *Giant*). The passages centered on the character of Thor Storm, the grizzled Nordic pioneer who became a candidate for the Alaska Territorial Legislature on a platform advocating Alaskan statehood, informing his granddaughter, Christine, about the legacy of Seattle and San Francisco cannery operators' exploitation of Alaska's fisheries. Her book had sold well and widely, though the movie adaptation would not do well in theaters. Nevertheless, *Ice Palace* had such an educational effect on the nation that it was referred to as "the Uncle Tom's Cabin of Alaska Statehood."

But the final vote on Alaskan statehood was held up by Representative Howard Smith, chairman of the Rules Committee, who stated:

I am opposed to statehood for Alaska. I am opposed to statehood for Hawaii, I am opposed to both of them together, I am opposed to them separately. I am opposed to bringing in Puerto Rico, which has been promised statehood by both of the great political parties like these two outlying Territories have. I am opposed to Puerto Rico, I am opposed to the Virgin Islands, I am opposed to all of them. I want to keep the United States of America on the American Continent. I hope I have made my position clear.

The statehood bill was brought to a vote after some political wrangling. It was ushered past the Rules Committee when it was was brought up on "privileged status" and put to a vote taken by roll call. It passed 217–172. The Senate, in turn, passed the House version by a 64–20 margin, and then the House passed the bill by a vote of 210–166. At last, on January 3, 1959, President Eisenhower signed the official declaration that made Alaska the forty-ninth state, leaving Hawaii to be the fiftieth.

So as your car, powered perhaps by gas from Alaskan oil, moves along a street that is unmarred by a Soviet bombing that never happened, so that you can go to buy your wild Alaskan salmon or king crab for dinner, and you look at your gold watch which might have Alaskan gold in it to see if you're on time, you can thank men like William Seward for helping to make it all happen.

Chronology

41,000 BCE Ice Age nears its peak, Beringia land bridge between Siberia and Alaska opens.

13,000 BCE Definite archaeological evidence proves that humans are living in Alaska by this time, though they may have been here earlier.

9000 BCE Ice Age recedes; ocean levels rise; Beringia floods, becoming the Bering Strait.

1728 Vitus Bering discovers the strait that is now named after him, the Bering Strait, but does not sight the Alaskan shoreline.

1741 Bering and Chirikov discover southern Alaskan coast and Aleutian Islands.

1775 Spanish explorer Juan Francisco de la Bodega y Quadra claims Baranof Island and Prince of Wales Island for Spain while searching for the Northwest Passage.

1783 The first permanent Russian settlement is founded at Three Saints Harbor.

1788 British explorer James Cook discovers the western coast of Alaska up through the Bering Strait to the ice pack; claims site of Anchorage for Britain.

1792 The settlement at Three Saints Harbor is moved to St. Paul's Harbor. This community will continue and eventually become the city of Kodiak.

1799 The Russian-American Company forms to represent the Imperial Russian monopoly on trade in the Alaska Territory.

1839 The Royal Saxon runs the British blockade on the Pearl River, and the Chinese Navy comes to its defense; First Opium War begins.

1842 The Treaty of Nanking opens up more trade with China for European nations.

1848 Geologist Petr Doroshin finds gold traces in a stream but doesn't think it's worth pursuing as a profitable venture.

1853 Turkey declares war on Russia; England and France also declare war on Russia; Crimean War begins.

1854 The "Charge of the Light Brigade" of the British against the Russian artillery emplacements highlights British military flaws; sentiment among British and French citizens turns against the Crimean War.

1856 Crimean War ends.

1858 Treaty of Aigun cedes the Chinese land between the Stanovoy Mountains and the Amur River to Russia.

1859 Russian diplomats attempt to institute sale of Alaska Territory to the United States, but the current administration is more interested in domestic issues.

1860 The 1860 Convention of Peking sees China cede parts of Outer Mongolia to Russia, including land on the Pacific Coast.

1861 Abraham Lincoln is sworn in as sixteenth president of the United States of America on March 4. William Seward is appointed secretary of state on March 5.

1861 At 4:30 a.m. on April 12, Confederates under General Pierre Beauregard open fire on Fort Sumter in Charleston, South Carolina. The American Civil War begins.

1865 On April 9, General Robert E. Lee surrenders his Confederate Army to General Ulysses S. Grant at the Appomattox Court House in Virginia, and on April 18, Confederate General Joseph E. Johnston surrenders to General Sherman near Durham in North Carolina. The remaining Confederate forces surrender by May, ending the American Civil War at a cost of over 620,000 Americans dead, 50,000 known amputees surviving, and many more wounded heading home.

1866 Eduard de Stoeckl and William Seward begin negotiations on the sale of the Alaska Territory to the United States.

1867 On March 30, President Johnson signs the treaty for the United States to purchase the Alaska Territory from Russia.

1868 In July, Congress approves and authorizes payment to Russia of $7.2 million for the Alaska Territory. On October 18, soldiers of the United States Army take formal possession of the Alaska Territory from the Russian garrison in Sitka.

1869 The gold strike at Sumdum becomes the first profitable gold strike in Alaska, the mines remaining profitable until World War II.

1878 The first fish cannery opens in Alaska at Klawock, making Alaskan-based fishing a profitable industry.

1880 Joe Juneau and Richard Harris strike gold in Gold Creek near modern-day Juneau, inspiring increased mineral exploration in the north.

1883 Army expedition of Frederick Schwatka, who travels through the Chilkoot Pass, then down the Yukon to St. Michael, and describes much of the interior of eastern Alaska.

1886 Howard Franklin discovers gold in Fortymile River, starting the first rush to interior Alaska and setting the stage for further strikes throughout the region.

1898 Congress finally allows the 1862 Homestead Act to apply to the Alaska Territory, opening up free land for settlers.

1903 Gold discoveries at Valdez Creek near modern-day Denali Highway inspire a rush by the late 1980s and 1990s.

1911 Kennecott copper mines begin production.

1939 United States investment in Alaska Territory strengthened by the building of naval bases at Sitka, Dutch Harbor, and Kodiak.

1942 Japanese forces attack the naval base at Dutch Harbor and occupy the islands of Attu and Kiska.

1951 Construction started on facilities and infrastructure for the Aircraft Control and Warning (AC&W) System to track and intercept hostile Soviet aircraft.

1954 Construction started on new facilities (and upgrades of some existing AC&W facilities) for the improved Distant Early Warning (DEW) system to track and intercept Soviet bombers and naval craft, as well as provide early warning in the case of a Soviet amphibious or paratroop invasion.

1957 The first major Alaska oil deposit is discovered at Swanson River on the Kenai Peninsula.

1959 Alaska officially becomes the forty-ninth state in the Union on January 3.

1964 A 9.2 magnitude earthquake strikes Alaska.

1968 North America's largest oil field is discovered in Prudhoe Bay (production begins in 1977).

Glossary

Aleut The Russian name for Natives of the Aleutian Islands and the western portion of the Alaska Peninsula, who call themselves the Unangas and the Sugpiaq and traditionally used kayaks to hunt seals, sea otters, whales, sea lions, and sometimes walrus.

annexation The act of adding another area, such as a country or territory, to an already established country, city, or state.

appropriation The act of setting money aside for an identified purpose, as by government officials for funding government business.

Arctic Circle An imaginary circle of latitude located about 1,650 miles (2,655 km) from the North Pole.

atomic bomb A destructive bomb whose power is generated by the splitting of atoms, which creates a large explosion.

creole (Alaskan) A person of mixed Russian and Native (usually Aleut) descent.

drainage (of a river) An area or district drained, including all rivers, lakes, ponds, and streams that flow out through some specific place (a river mouth, for example) before hitting some other body of water.

enfranchise To admit those in a territory/municipality to the rights and privileges of the citizenry, and especially to the right of voting for their government.

expedition A journey undertaken, usually with a specific goal, such as research or exploration.

fishery A company, as well as an industry, that harvests and sells fish, shrimp, lobster, etc.

fjord A long, narrow area of the sea located between steep cliffs.

glacier A large mass of ice that travels slowly, formed by an accumulation of snow.

gold strike To discover gold during the course of drilling, mining, or prospecting.

homesteader A person who settled under the US Homestead Act.

ice pack A large expanse of ice created by the pushing together of individual ice sheets by water and wind.

impeachment To charge a public official with a crime or misdemeanor, usually with the aim to remove them from office.

imperial Relating to an empire or an emperor.

imperialism A policy in which a country gains power by taking control of other areas.

kayak A long, pointed boat that is powered by a paddle with a blade on each end.

lobbyist (political) A person or group of people who try to influence specific government decisions.

maritime Located near or next to the sea, or relating to sailing on the sea or doing business (such as trading) by sea

mining The process or business of digging in mines to obtain minerals, coal, metals, jewels, etc.

monopoly Total control of goods or services within a specific area.

navigator A person who determines their current position on the globe, and then can determine the correct course (direction) for a ship, airplane, etc. to get to a desired location from the current position.

Northwest Passage A fabled water route once believed to exist in North America that would link the Atlantic and Pacific Oceans.

oil field An area rich in petroleum deposits that is often exploited for commercial gain.

opium A reddish-brown drug derived from the opium poppy; used as both as a recreational drug and for medical purposes.

Ottoman Empire A former Turkish empire spanning Southeastern Europe, West Asia, and Northern Africa, at its largest including Turkey, Syria, Iraq, Lebanon, Israel, Palestine, the Saudi Arabian Peninsula, Egypt, the Barbary States, the Balkans, and parts of Russia and Hungary.

penal colony A remote area used to house convicts; often located on an island.

relinquish To give up, or to give power over something, to another individual or group.

sound (maritime) A long, wide inlet running parallel to the coast; or a long waterway that connects two larger bodies of water, or that separates an island from the mainland.

survey To measure and record the features of an area, often for use in creating a map.

strait A narrow waterway connecting one large body of water to another.

tsar The title of the hereditary ruler of the Russian Empire before the 1917 Russian Revolution.

tundra A level or flat area, located in northern regions, with no trees and where the ground remains frozen year-round.

war footing Being prepared to start or continue a war.

Further Information

Books

Brinkley, Douglas. *The Quiet World: Saving Alaska's Wilderness Kingdom*, 1879–1960. New York: HarperCollins Publishers, 2011.

Devine, Bob. *Alaska: A Visual Tour of America's Great Land.* Des Moines, IA: National Geographic, 2014.

Stahr, Walter. *Seward: Lincoln's Indispensable Man.* New York: Simon & Schuster, 2012.

Websites

Meeting of Frontiers

international.loc.gov/intldl/mtfhtml/mfovrvw.html

The Meeting of Frontiers, a digital library created in partnership between Russia and the US, examines the histories of Russia's eastward and America's westward expansion, including their meeting in Alaska. The collection is available in both English and Russian and houses thousands of items, including photographs, maps, sound recordings, and more.

Shared Beringian Heritage Program

www.nps.gov/akso/beringia

The Shared Beringian Heritage Program explores the unique culture, natural resources, and Native customs shared between Russia and the United States in the Bering Strait area.

Museums and Parks

The Bering Land Bridge National Preserve: A Bridge to the Past, Present, and Future

www.nps.gov/bela/index.htm

The Bering Land Bridge National Preserve protects a small portion of the historic land bridge. Learn about the indigenous flora and fauna, and the stories of the first people to cross the Bering Land Bridge.

Cordova Historical Museum

www.cordovamuseum.org

The Cordova Historical Museum works to preserve the history and culture of the Alaskan town of Cordova and the surrounding area. The museum includes exhibits on Native culture, the fishing industry, and more.

Sheldon Museum & Cultural Center

www.sheldonmuseum.org

Visit the Sheldon Museum, located in Haines, Alaska. This museum houses several exhibits that celebrate local history, including Tlingit culture, mining and fishing, and more.

Sitka Historical Museum

www.sitkahistory.org

Sitka Historical Museum features photographs, artifacts, and archives covering the Native, Russian, and American history of the area.

Sitka National Historical Park

www.nps.gov/sitk/index.htm

Located on the western coast of Baranof Island, at Sitka National Park, visitors explore historic sites and artifacts from Alaska's past that examine the past influences of Natives, Russians, and Americans in this area.

Bibliography

Andrews, C. L. "Alaska under the Russians: Baranof the Builder." *The Washington Historical Quarterly*, Vol. 7, No. 3 (July 1916): 202–216.

Bailey, Thomas A. "Why the United States Purchased Alaska." *Pacific Historical Review*, Vol. 3, No. 1 (March 1934): 39–49.

Bancroft, Hubert Howe. *History of Alaska. 1730–1885.* San Francisco, CA: A. L. Bancroft & Company, 1886.

Brinkley, Douglas. *The Quiet World: Saving Alaska's Wilderness Kingdom, 1879-1960.* New York: HarperCollins Publishers, 2011.

Brooks, Alfred H. "The Value of Alaska." *Geographical Review*, Vol. 15, No. 1 (January 1925): 25–50.

Coates, Ken. "Controlling the Periphery: The Territorial Administration of the Yukon and Alaska, 1867-1959." *The Pacific Northwest Quarterly*, Vol. 78, No. 4 (Oct. 1987) : 145–151.

Dixon, E. James. "Cultural Chronology of Central Interior Alaska." *Arctic Anthropology*, Vol. 22, No. 1 (1985): 47–66.

Gerus, Oleh W. "The Russian Withdrawal from Alaska: The Decision to Sell." *Revista de Historia de América*, No. 75/76 (Jan–Dec 1973): 157–178.

Golder, Frank A. "The Purchase of Alaska." *The American Historical Review*, Vol. 25, No. 3 (April 1920): 411–425.

Griffin, Dennis. "A Culture in Transition: A History of Acculturation and Settlement Near the Mouth of the Yukon River, Alaska." *Arctic Anthropology*, Vol. 33, No. 1 (1996): 98–115.

Hinckley, Ted C. "William H. Seward Visits His Purchase." *Oregon Historical Quarterly*, Vol. 72, No. 2 (June 1971): 127–147.

Hulley, Clarence C. "A Historical Survey of the Matanuska Valley Settlement in Alaska." *The Pacific Northwest Quarterly*, Vol. 40, No. 4 (Oct 1949): 327–340.

Hummel, Laurel J. "The U.S. Military as Geographical Agent: The Case of Cold War Alaska." *Geographical Review*, Vol. 95, No. 1 (Jan 2005): 47–72.

Kushner, Howard I. "'Seward's Folly'?: American Commerce in Russian America and the Alaska Purchase." *California Historical Quarterly*, Vol. 54, No. 1 (Spring 1975): 4–26.

The Library of Congress, *Meeting of Frontiers*, Joint US/Russian information collaboration. international.loc.gov/intldl/mtfhtml/mfovrvw.html

Luthin, Reinhard H. "The Sale of Alaska." *The Slavonic and East European Review*, Vol. 16, No. 46 (July 1937): 168–182.

McCrisken, Trevor B. "Exceptionalism: Manifest Destiny." In *Encyclopedia of American Foreign Policy*, edited by Richard

Dean Burns, Alexander DeConde, and Fredrik Logevall.
2nd. ed. Vol. 2. New York: Charles Scribner's Sons, 2002.

Ray, Dorothy Jean. "Nineteenth Century Settlement
and Subsistence Patterns in Bering Strait." *Arctic
Anthropology*, Vol. 2, No. 2 (1964): 61–94.

Sharrow, Walter G. "William Henry Seward and the Basis for
American Empire, 1850–1860." *Pacific Historical Review*,
Vol. 36, No. 3 (August 1967): 325–342.

Smith, Theodore Clarke. "Expansion after the Civil War,
1865–71." *Political Science Quarterly*, Vol. 16, No. 3
(Sept 1901): 412-436.

Stahr, Walter. *Seward: Lincoln's Indispensable Man.* New
York, NY: Simon & Schuster, 2012.

Stone, Kirk H. "Populating Alaska: The United States Phase."
Geographical Review, Vol. 42, No. 3 (July 1952): 384–404.

United States. Congress. Senate.; *Journal of the executive
proceedings of the Senate of the United States of
America* (Volume 17); Printed by order of the Senate of
the United States (Washington, DC: US GPO), 1828.

Van Deusen, Glyndon G. "The Life and Career of William
Henry Seward 1801-1872." *University of Rochester
Library Bulletin*, Volume XXXI, Number 1 (Autumn
1978): 3–21.

Zakaria, Fareed; "The Myth of America's 'Free Security.'" *World
Policy Journal*, Vol. 14, No. 2 (Summer, 1997): 35–43.

Index

Page numbers in **boldface** are illustrations. Entries in **boldface** are glossary terms.

About the Author

Hex Kleinmartin, PhD, has taught anthropology and history, worked on many archaeological excavations, and undertaken a number of instances of historical research. He has written several books and papers on subjects ranging from archaeological site reports and specialized analyses of archaeological items found on them, to the brief histories of states and their important figures. He enjoys both teaching and learning, and tries to do plenty of both with an anthropological view to help keep things in context.